HOW TO DESIGN
THE WORLD'S BEST
ROBOT

IN 10 SIMPLE STEPS

PAUL MASON

WAYLAND

Published in Great Britain in 2018 by Wayland

Editor: Nicola Edwards
Design: Kevin Knight

Artwork by Tim Hutchinson

ISBN: 978 0 7502 9946 6
10 9 8 7 6 5 4 3 2 1

Wayland, an imprint of
Hachette Children's Group
Part of Hodder and Stoughton
Carmelite House
50 Victoria Embankment
London EC4Y 0DZ

An Hachette UK Company
www.hachette.co.uk
www.hachettechildrens.co.uk

Printed and bound in China

Picture acknowledgements:
All photographic images courtesy of Shutterstock
except p10 (m) Alamy; p13 (l) Getty Images; p13 (r) Alamy;
p16 Wikimedia Commons; p30 Wikimedia Commons

CONTENTS

DESIGNING THE BEST EVER ROBOT

If the news is true, soon there will be a robot for every job. We will be travelling in robot cars. When we get ill, nanobots will make us better. Robot servants will help around the house. Kids might even be taught by robot teachers. It seems there is nothing robots won't be able to do for us.

DESIGN YOUR OWN ROBOT

Imagine being able to design your OWN robot. What kind of jobs would it help you with? ('Homework' is not allowed as an answer...) Once you had decided what the robot was for, how would you go about designing it? What kind of decisions would you have to make as part of the design process?

Research Note

Robots are machines that do work for humans. The word 'robot' comes from the Czech Republic. There, *robota* means 'forced labour'. When the idea of machines that could work for us became popular, 'robot' seemed like a good name.

Not a robot car – robots making a car! This is a Fiat engine factory.

RESEARCHING ROBOTS

The first thing you would need to do is some research. You might think you know what robots can do – but are your ideas right?

WORK IT OUT!

Find out about the jobs robots can do. Research this in three stages:

1) Gather as much information as you can:

Using at least three different Internet search engines, find out as much as you can about actual, real-life robots. You could search for:

• Top ten robots
• New + robots + [the current year: e.g. '+ 2017']
• Best robot

2) Sort through the information: Read through the information and put aside anything that seems unreliable. Unreliable information often:

• contains lots of spelling mistakes
• does not make sense
• does not tell you when it was written or who wrote it

3) Organise the information: Finally, organise the remaining information into groups. This will help you find what you need later. For example, your groups could be 'how robots move', 'robot jobs' and 'friend robots'.

THE DESIGN BRIEF

Once your research is finished, you can start to work out a 'design brief'. All designs start with one of these. It is a description of what the design has to do. For example, the design brief for a hairdryer might include: 'Must have hot and cold settings.' If the hairdryer ends up blowing only COLD air, the design has failed. A final design that does everything in the design brief is a success.

The world's worst hairdryer? This product's designer didn't think enough about the brief!

DESIGN BRIEF: WHAT IS THIS ROBOT FOR?

People have always imagined robots as helpers. A robot's job is to make human life easier. The robot in this book will be exactly that: a robot helper, named Mia. It will be designed to be used in hospitals, especially as a robot friend for sick children. The robot will then be loaded with software for particular jobs.

WORK IT OUT!

What skills would a hospital robot need? You need to work this out so the skills can be included in the design brief.

Below is a list of things the robot is going to help with. Try to work out any skills the robot will need to do these jobs. Some skills for job 1 have been filled in as an example:

Job	Skills needed
Deliver food and drink to patients	Moving around; selecting objects; passing objects to patients; possibly speaking and listening.
Give patients drugs	
Explain treatments to patients	
Provide patients (especially children) with company and entertainment	

Check your ideas on page 31.

Research Note

'Robots' first appeared in a play called Rossum's Universal Robots, in 1920. In the play, robots were mass-produced workers. They could easily be mistaken for humans, but could not feel emotions or think for themselves. Ever since, people have imagined robots as helpers whose job is to make life easier for the humans.

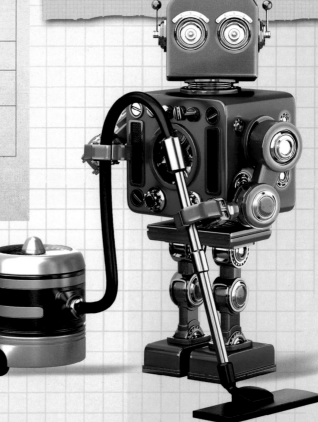

A robot to help with vacuuming has been a popular idea since at least the 1950s.

WORK IT OUT!

There are more things to consider before starting the design. Get into a group with at least two other people to discuss:

1) Do you think the robot's appearance is important? For example, would it matter if a hospital robot had a blank expression? (Remember, the robot will be working with sick children.)

2) Does the robot need to be strong? To be strong it would also have to be heavy and large. (Hint: base your decision on the jobs it will be doing.)

3) How large and expensive should the robot be? Would one big, expensive robot be better than six smaller, less expensive ones?

You can check your ideas on page 31.

FINAL DESIGN BRIEF

The work it out! panels will have given you some ideas for the final design brief. These will probably include among the robot's skills:

- Move about
  - Move objects
    - Recognise objects and people
    - Speak and listen
    - Process information
      - Sense the world around it
        - Look and act like a friend
          - Be small and inexpensive

Your research (see page 5) will have given you some ideas about how this design brief could be turned into an actual robot. For example, some robots move on wheels, while others can actually walk. Before sketching your design, think about which is best for your bot.

This robot – which you would not want to tread on your toes – is humanoid, even though it does not look like a living, breathing human.

STEP 1

SKETCH A DESIGN

The next step is to sketch a design. This is where the designer can use his or her imagination. The only rule is that the robot has to do everything on the design brief. Apart from that, this first design can be based on anything you discovered during the robot research phase (see page 5).

Height: 150cm

Mia has a human shape
The skin on Mia's face and hands looks human. Mia needs to help patients relax. Looking and moving around like a human nurse will make this more likely.

Microphones inside mouth and ears
Ear microphones allow Mia to hear what people are saying.
Mouth microphone for replies, to make Mia seem as human as possible.

Main computer processors inside upper chest.
Powerful computers will control all Mia's functions.

Medicine store and entertainment system
Patients can download music, games, box sets, etc.

Titanium skeleton

Head contains cameras and image-processing equipment
Mia will be able to recognise patients, drugs and locations.

Charging point
Information download/upload socket

Hands have joints at the wrist and knuckles

Human-like hands will let Mia pick up and put down even small objects, such as pills.

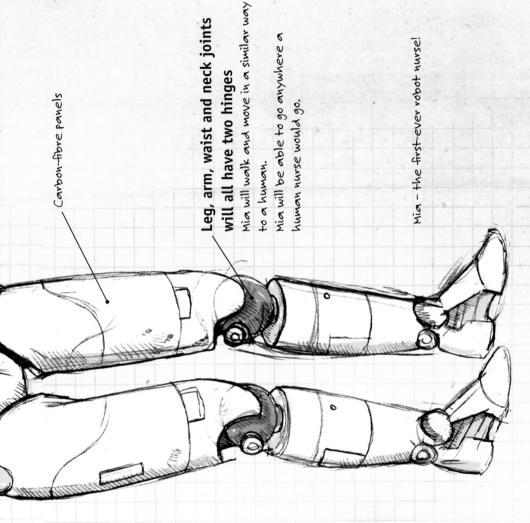

Carbon-fibre panels

Leg, arm, waist and neck joints will all have two hinges

Mia will walk and move in a similar way to a human.

Mia will be able to go anywhere a human nurse would go.

Mia – the first-ever robot nurse!

Electric batteries at lower rear

Putting the heavy batteries low down will make sure Mia does not topple over.

TESTING THE DESIGN

The next step in designing Mia is to test each part of the design. You have to ask whether the robot can actually be made that way? You also need to check if there is actually a better way to do the same thing. Better can mean something that works better. It can also mean something that works just as well, but costs less.

WORK IT OUT!

Does the design shown here do everything in the design brief?

Hospital bot design brief

Robot should:

Move about

Move objects

Recognise objects and people

Speak and listen

Process information

Sense the world around it

Look and act like a friend

Be small and inexpensive

Not all robots are humanoid – in fact, most robots in existence today are not. So one of the first decisions to make is whether hospital bot Mia actually needs to be human shaped at all.

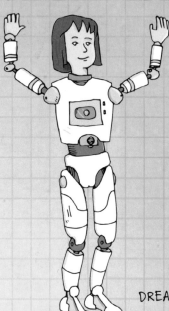

DREAM DESIGN

ALTERNATIVE DESIGNS

Mia has to be able to move around. This means the main alternative shape for the robot would be a tractor robot. These can scoot along the floor quickly, and with a flat top it would be good for fetching and carrying. Tractor bots are also cheaper and easier to build than humanoid robots.

Tractor-bots are sometimes used for bomb disposal.

Research Note

Tractor bots come in different shapes and sizes. Most are small, relatively simple and inexpensive. They are used for lots of jobs, from bomb disposal and exploring poisonous areas to vacuuming and lawn cutting.

• Many tractor bots have a flexible arm that can pick up small objects.

• Tractor bots normally have at least one camera.

• Some tractor bots are controlled by a human, using remote control. Bomb-disposal tractor bots are an example of this.

• Other tractor bots are controlled by onboard computers, which can sense the world around them. Robot vacuum cleaners (bottom left) are an example.

Tractor bots are not usually able to communicate with humans.

WORK IT OUT!

Which is best, a tractor robot or a humanoid robot?

To decide, look at the jobs the robot has to do and the skills it will need. These are:

Job	Humanoid	Tractor
Deliver food and drink to patients	1	1
Give patients drugs		
Explain treatments to patients		
Provide patients with company and entertainment		

Skills	Humanoid	Tractor
Move about	1	1
Move objects		
Recognise objects and people		
Speak and listen		
Process information		
Sense the world around it		
Look and act friendly		
Be small and inexpensive		

Give each type of robot a score of one point, based on what it would be good at. For example, both should be able to deliver food and drink, so for that category they each get one point.

There are a maximum of 12 points available. The robot shape that scores highest is the best one.

You can check your answers on page 31.

THE FINAL DESIGN

The final decision is that a humanoid robot is best. Because tractor bots do not usually communicate with humans, it would not be able to do some of Mia's most important jobs. A tractor bot would probably also not have some of the skills that would be needed in hospital.

DESIGN THE ROBOT'S FACE

What should Mia's face look like? The original design is for a human-looking robot with robot 'skin' on its hands and face. Is this possible? And if it IS possible, is human skin the best design for Mia and the humans it will be working with?

Mia is planned to have a human face – but can it be convincingly human?

DREAM DESIGN

ANDROID SKIN

Robots designed to look like humans are called androids. The original design for Mia is an android. Recently, several androids with 'skin' have actually been made. You need to decide whether these robots would fall into category 1), 2) or 3) from the research note below.

Research Note

Robotics experts think that whether we like a robot depends on how human it seems:

1) People like human-shaped robots that are obviously NOT human

2) People dislike robots that try to look like real humans but fail

3) People like robots that successfully look human

The gap between 1 and 3 is sometimes called the 'uncanny valley'.

WORK IT OUT!

Research some famous human-looking robots with 'skin'. Try to decide whether they are uncanny.

Do Internet video searches for 'Albert Hubo robot', 'Erica robot' and 'Actroid-F and Kurokawa robots'. Give each robot a score out of three. 3 is totally uncanny (odd-looking and creepy), and 0 is not uncanny at all. Then get at least two of your friends to watch the videos and score the robots.

Finally, make an arithmetic mean of the scores. For example, if Albert Hubo scored 3, 2 and 1, the mean would be [3 + 2 + 1] ÷ 3 = 2

Do any of the robots score 0? This would mean that no one found them uncanny. That would mean it is possible to make a likeable android.

What score would you give each of these robot faces if 3 was for totally uncanny and 0 was for not uncanny at all?

THE FINAL DESIGN

Trying to make Mia an android with human-looking skin is risky and expensive. If the robot looks uncanny, patients will not like it. Mia might even scare the children it is meant to be helping.

The simplest and least expensive solution is to give the robot a friendly 'face', but made of plastic or metal. It will have something like eyes and a mouth, but without trying to look exactly like a human.

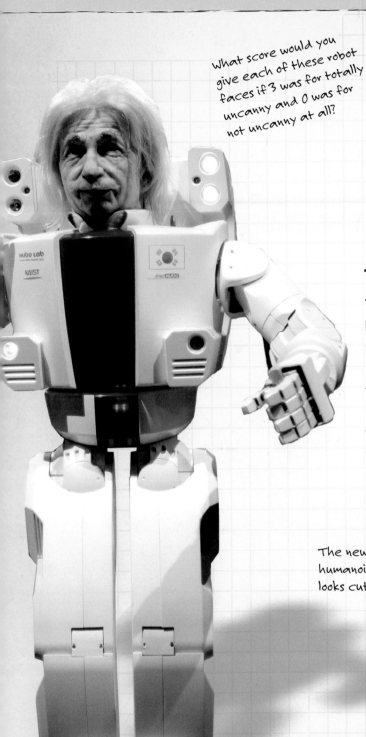

The new design's face is humanoid – but the robot looks cute, not creepy!

REVISED DESIGN

DECIDE HOW BIG THE ROBOT SHOULD BE

Mia is definitely going to be human-shaped – but what size should the robot be? The design brief says it should be 'small and inexpensive'. The original design was for a robot 1.5m tall: the size of a small grown-up. Does Mia need to be this big?

CHECK THE DESIGN BRIEF

The design brief has other information
that will help you work out the robot's
ideal height. The three most relevant
bits are ticked:

✗ Move about
✔ Move objects
✗ Recognise objects and people
✗ Speak and listen
✗ Process information
✗ Sense the world around it
✔ Look and act like a friend
✔ Be small and inexpensive

All the others are things that the robot
could do whatever size it was, but:
• A big robot would cost more to make
• A tiny robot would not be able to
put objects on patients' beds or
bedside tables
• A grown-up-sized robot would not
seem friend-like to children

SMALL – BUT HOW SMALL?

A smaller robot will cost less and seem
more like a friend to children. But if it is
too small, it will not be able to reach all
the places it needs to. You need to work
out the smallest size Mia could be.

180cms

150cms

DREAM DESIGN

WORK IT OUT!

How small could Mia be?

In most hospitals, the tables beside the beds are about 75cm high. Mia needs to be able to see the top of this table to put food, drink and drugs on it. The robot's chin needs to be higher than 75cm.

Mia is going to be humanoid. In most humans, the distance from their chin to the top of their head makes up 14% of their height. The other 86% is legs, body and neck.

Use this fact to work out the shortest Mia could be and still see on to hospital tables:

Height	86% of total height	Bedside table height	Difference
1.5m (original design)	129cm	0.75m	54cm
1.0m		0.75m	
0.9m		0.75m	
0.8m		0.75m	

You can check your answer on page 31.

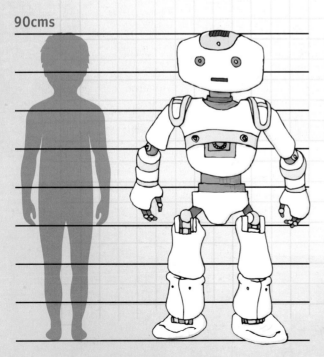

90cms

THE FINAL DESIGN

The final design is for Mia to be much smaller than first planned. The robot will be 90cm tall. This is about the height of a three-year-old child. It is a good size for making friends with children who are in hospital having treatment.

REVISED DESIGN

How is the robot going to move about? Should it have legs with wheels underneath, and move like a radio-controlled car? Or will the robot walk like a human, lifting one foot at a time?

Four parts of the design brief affect this decision. They are:
• Move about
• Deliver items to patients
• Look and act like a friend
• Be inexpensive

You have to decide three things:
1) Can both types of robot move about in a hospital, delivering things to patients?
2) Which type is more friend-like?
3) Which one is least expensive?

WORK IT OUT!

A robot that walks like a human would be able to go where the nurses and doctors go. Could a wheeled robot do the same?

To decide, look at the picture below and make a list of the ways humans move (or are moved) in hospitals. There are at least three. Do any of them use wheels? If so, a wheeled robot would be suitable.

You can check your ideas on page 31.

Research Note

The best robot walkers have four legs. There is one called Big Dog that can walk on icy ground, snow, mud and steep, slippery slopes. Robots with two legs are not as good on tricky surfaces, but they walk well on smooth ones.

Robots on wheels are cheaper and easier to build, but they need a flat, smooth surface and have to keep their wheels on the ground.

WORK IT OUT!

Would a wheeled robot make a good friend for sick kids?

Wheeled robots cannot lift their feet off the ground. They also have to keep their weight on their feet in case they fall over. They cannot lie down because it is difficult to get up again.

Spend an hour with one of your friends, doing normal things. Make a note every time you do something a wheeled robot could not do. Use your notes to decide whether a wheeled robot would make a good friend.

THE FINAL DESIGN

A wheeled robot would be able to move around delivering things, and costs less. A walking robot can move around too, and is a better robot friend. So the final design is for a robot that can be fitted with TWO systems, depending on which jobs the robot will be doing.

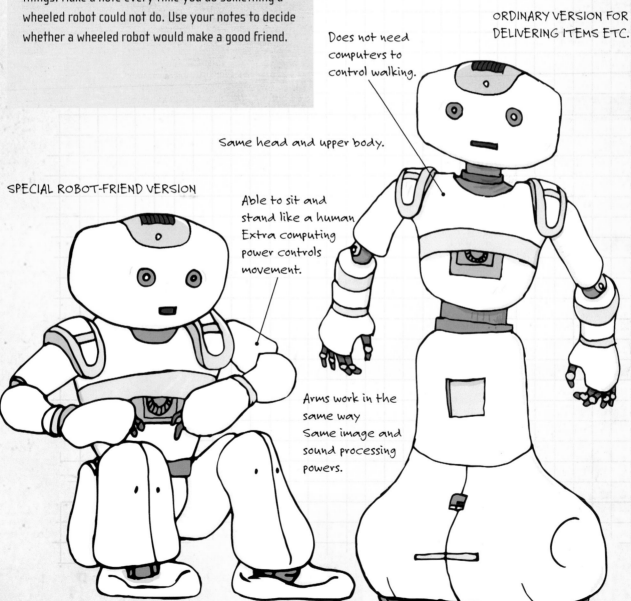

ORDINARY VERSION FOR DELIVERING ITEMS ETC.

Does not need computers to control walking.

Same head and upper body.

SPECIAL ROBOT-FRIEND VERSION

Able to sit and stand like a human Extra computing power controls movement.

Arms work in the same way Same image and sound processing powers.

HELP THE ROBOT SEE

To be able to move around safely, robot Mia needs to able to sense its surroundings. Otherwise it will bash into walls, tables and other obstacles. This would not be very relaxing for patients. Mia also has to be able to recognise people, so that each patient gets the right treatment.

THE ORIGINAL DESIGN

In the original design, Mia has two cameras for 'eyes'. The robot is also fitted with devices that can tell how far away objects are.

Mia has to recognise faces perfectly – otherwise patients might end up being given the wrong drugs. The software designers have asked you to suggest which measurements Mia's facial recognition software should use [see the research note below].

Left eye holds camera
for seeing objects less than 2m away

Right eye holds camera
Sees objects over 2m away

Throat (forward distance)

Left shoulder (distance to left)

Right shoulder (distance to right)

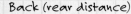

Back (rear distance)

Mia is fitted with
distance sensors

Research Note

Computers recognise people by recording the distances between different parts of their faces. Then the computer checks the distances against its database. If they match someone in the database, the computer can tell who that person is.

WORK IT OUT!

To come up with some facial recognition measurements, you need at least two friends. Take photos of your faces. (Make sure you each look straight at the camera and sit the exact-same distance from the lens.) Now start measuring! You could start with:

• the distance between your eyes

• how far your nose is above your chin

• how wide your nose is

Write down seven different results on a table like this:

Measurement	Friend 1	Friend 2	Friend 3
1 Eye to eye	14 mm		
2 Chin to nose	17 mm		
3 Nose width	10 mm		
4			
5			
6			
7			

Which five measurements have the biggest differences between each of you? These would be the best examples of measurements for software designers to use.

You can check your ideas on page 31.

THE FINAL DESIGN

The final design may end up looking different, but it will work the same way as the original. Mia's computer memory will store things it has seen – including faces, drugs, foods and drinks. Mia will use facial recognition software to 'learn' people's faces. Hospital staff will then be able to programme in the names, treatments and other needs of each patient in Mia's memory.

Distance sensors for 'eyes'

Back of head distance sensor

Camera in forehead

Camera 'mouth'

Right shoulder distance sensor

Left shoulder distance sensor

GET YOUR ROBOT TO PICK THINGS UP

Picking up objects is one of the most important skills Mia needs. If the robot is taking medicine to patients, for example, it has to pick up trays of pills. It also needs to be able to deliver drinks and food. Mia has to do these jobs without crushing the objects it is picking up.

DREAM DESIGN

DESIGN CHALLENGES

In the original design, Mia had four fingers and a thumb. The robot's hand looked just like a human one. There are two problems with this:

1) Human fingers have three joints and lots of muscles to move them. Making a robot hand that works the same way would be very expensive.

2) Mia is now going to be much smaller. It would be impossible to make a human-style robot hand small enough to match the rest of Mia's body.

Mia's hand has to be redesigned smaller and less expensive. Fewer fingers would make it smaller and less expensive to build. But how few?

Research Note

Robot hands are fitted with pressure sensors. These tell the robot's computer how much force it is using to hold an object.

The robot's computer software stores pictures of objects – for example, an orange. The software also has instructions about how hard each object should be gripped. The software makes sure the robot does not grip an orange as hard as it would a baseball.

Getting the robot's grip right will be important for the safety of the hospital's fruit supplies!

WORK IT OUT!

How many fingers (and thumbs) does Mia really need? You can work this out using your own hand to pick up various objects.

You need:

- Little paper cup with small sweets in it
- Sandwich
- Glass of water
- Large orange

Try picking each of these up using 1) Only your fingers 2) One finger and one thumb 3) Two fingers and a thumb 4) Three fingers and a thumb.

Record your results in a table. Mark a Y (yes) or N (no) to show whether you could pick up the object and hold it securely. Use the results to decide the best number of fingers for Mia.

You can check your results on page 31.

Mia's almost-human skin has been replaced with a proper robot hand. This has two fewer fingers.

THE FINAL DESIGN

The final design is for a cheaper, less complicated hand than the original. It will have two fingers and a thumb. The robot will still be able to pick up medicines, food and drinks. It can also use one finger to push buttons controlling other machines.

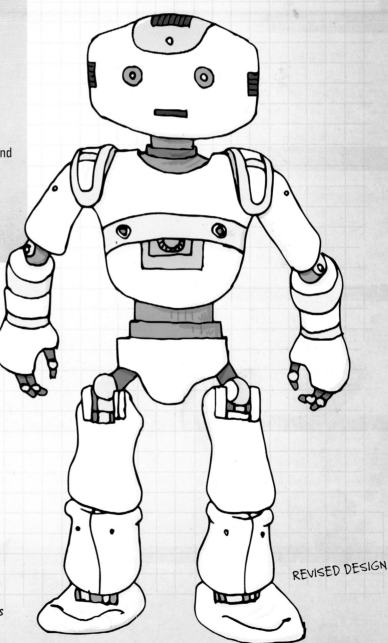

REVISED DESIGN

Part of Mia's job is explaining treatments to patients, so the robot needs to be able to say things like: "(Name of Patient), please take these pills." Mia also has to be able to listen to a patient's reply. For example, Mia might ask: "Are you thirsty?" If the patient says yes, Mia will fetch a drink. If no, the robot will move on to the next patient.

DREAM DESIGN

The original design had microphones where humans have ears, and a speaker as a mouth.

SOUND DIRECTION

Mia needs to be able to tell where sounds are coming from. This will let the robot turn its head and look at whoever is speaking to it – just like a human. (To understand how important this is, try speaking to someone who is deliberately NOT looking at you.)

Research Note

Voice commands are used to control many computers. Telephone systems can recognise simple numbers, and words such as 'yes' and 'no'. Many smartphones and tablets have voice recognition software. This allows you to ask important questions such as, "What haircut does Justin Beiber have today?" or give commands like, "Show me funny videos of cats."

WORK IT OUT!

How can Mia be programmed to know where sounds are coming from? You need your whole class to work this out.

One person stands in the middle wearing a blindfold. Then everyone else makes a big circle around him or her. Someone calls out the player in the middle's name. The player then has to point at whoever spoke.

Try this 10 times, with the calls coming from all around the circle. Every time the player gets it right, they score a point.

Now do the same thing again – but with the player wearing a wax earplug in one ear. Compare the scores. What do they tell you about how we hear where sounds are coming from?

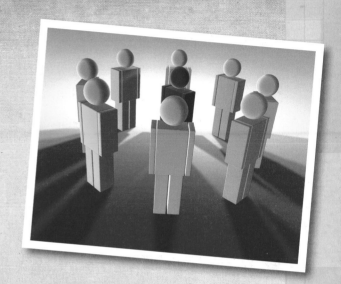

THE FINAL DESIGN

Most people do much better at the game using both ears. This is because our brains work out whether sounds have arrived at our ears at different times. If a sound reaches our left ear before our right ear, for example, we know the sound comes from the left.

Mia's software can be programmed to behave the same way. The robot will know when sound has reached its microphones, and use the information to work out where the sound has come from.

In the final design, Mia will have four microphones. There will be one on each side. These will help Mia work out exactly who is speaking. The robot will also have two speaking microphones, one on each side of its head. This is so that Mia's 'voice' can be in stereo. Most humans prefer stereo sounds to mono from a single speaker. The difference is like listening to music using earbuds, then taking one out.

Left microphone

Left speaker

Right microphone

Right speaker

REVISED DESIGN

PICK YOUR MATERIALS

One of a designer's most important decisions is about materials. Picking the best materials can make the difference between a good design and a poor one. That is why people sometimes describe a poor design as a 'chocolate teapot'. (Imagine what would happen the first time you tried to make tea in a teapot made of chocolate...)

ORIGINAL DESIGN

The original design is for a robot with a titanium skeleton. The main body panels are carbon fibre. These two materials are lightweight and flexible. Being lightweight will mean the robot does not use much power, and can easily be moved by people at the hospital. Being flexible will mean the robot is less likely to be damaged if it is accidentally bashed or knocked over.

Getting the materials wrong would mean Mia ended up being as much use as a chocolate teapot.

Research Note

Titanium and carbon fibre offer strength and flexibility. They are used to make many products, including Tour de France bicycles, aircraft, racing yachts, MotoGP bikes and Formula 1 cars.

Titanium and carbon are both unusual materials that are difficult to work with. This makes them expensive:

• Titanium parts cost £150.00 per kg (compared to aluminium at £50.00 per kg)

• Carbon fibre parts cost £75.00 per kg (compared to 3-D printed plastic at £10.00 per kg)

DESIGN PROBLEMS

There is a problem with the original design. Titanium and carbon fibre both cost a lot of money. The design brief says Mia has to be 'inexpensive', not expensive! You need to work out how much could be saved by using less-expensive materials.

WORK IT OUT!

Mia will weigh 4.5kg. This is made up of three main things:

1) Titanium skeleton: 1.8kg

2) Carbon-fibre body panels: 1.2kg

3) Computers, sensors, etc: 1.5kg

Look at the information about costs in the research note on page 24. Use it to work out how much you could save by using aluminium and plastic instead of titanium and carbon fibre. Record the results in a table like the one on the right.

Titanium	Aluminium	Cost difference
150 x 1.8 = £270		

Carbon Fibre	Plastic	Cost difference

You can check your results on page 31.

THE FINAL DESIGN

The final design will use aluminium and plastic as a way of saving money. In total, using these different materials will reduce the cost of making Mia by £258.00. This will make it easier to sell the robot at a price hospitals can afford.

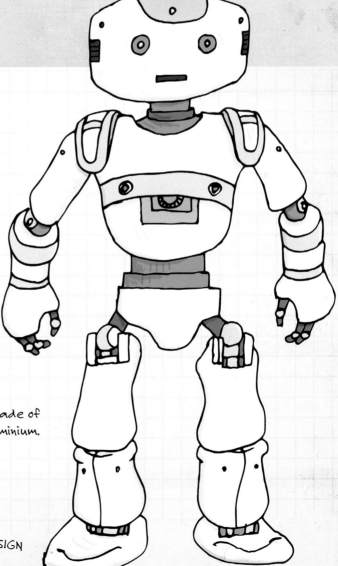

Plastic body panels are 3-D printed.

Mia's skeleton is made of lightweight aluminium.

REVISED DESIGN

CUSTOMISING YOUR ROBOT

Mia will have lots of functions built in. The basic robot will be able to move about, pick things up and carry them, see, listen and speak, and do all the other jobs that were part of the design brief. This basic model could be customised using special apps. Then it could perform other jobs, too.

MIA – CLASSROOM ASSISTANT

Mia could help humans in lots of ways. For example, the robot could be a brilliant classroom assistant. Imagine if you were finding a subject difficult. You could go off for a special lesson with the class robot. If Mia had a touchscreen on its chest, you could even do test exercises with some robot help.

MIA – PERSONAL ASSISTANT

Part of the design brief for Mia was to work well with children. This is partly why it is the same size as a small child. Imagine if Mia was your own robot personal assistant. What kind of things could Mia help you with?

Research Note

App is short for application. In computing, an app is a piece of software that does a specific job. For example, there are apps that turn a phone or tablet into a radio. There are apps for surfers to check whether the waves are good at their local beach. There are even apps that tell you where your dog has been on its walk.

Which picture shows a Viking longship?

Lessons on Viking culture – from a robot!

WORK IT OUT!

Make a timeline of things you do at home each day. Could a robot personal assistant help? If so, what apps would the robot need?

Your timeline might start like the table opposite.

Carry on the timeline when you get home. At the end you will have a list of apps that need to be loaded on to your robot assistant's computer.

Time	Activity	Help from Mia	App required
7.15	Wake up	Alarm (use favourite J Bieber song)	Date/time app Music app
7.30	Breakfast		
7.45	Shower, get dressed	Warn about rain or other weather for day	Weather app
8.00	Leave for school		

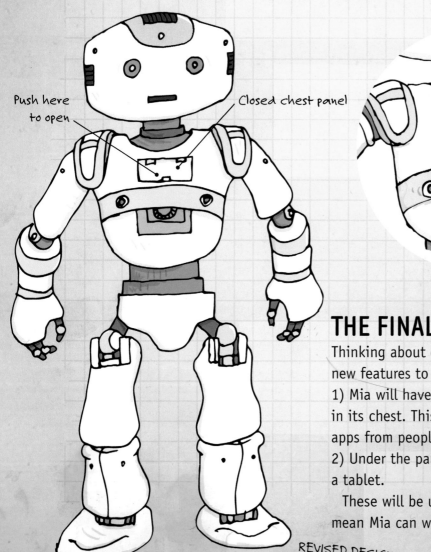

Push here to open

Closed chest panel

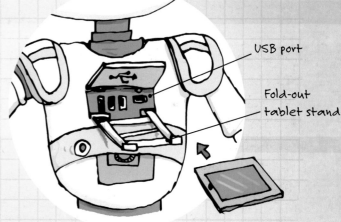

USB port

Fold-out tablet stand

THE FINAL DESIGN

Thinking about other uses for Mia has added two new features to the robot's design:

1) Mia will have an extra USB socket under a panel in its chest. This will make it easy to download apps from people's smartphones and tablets.

2) Under the panel will also be a clip for attaching a tablet.

These will be useful in the hospital, but will mean Mia can work in other places too.

REVISED DESIGN

THE WORLD'S BEST ROBOT?

The key parts of Mia's original design have now been checked. You know whether they could have been designed better, and have changed anything that could be improved. The shape, size and skills of the robot have all been decided. The basic design is finished.

Mia still has a human shape

The robot no longer has human-looking skin. Research said that a humanoid robot that still looked like a robot would be most popular.

Height: 90cm

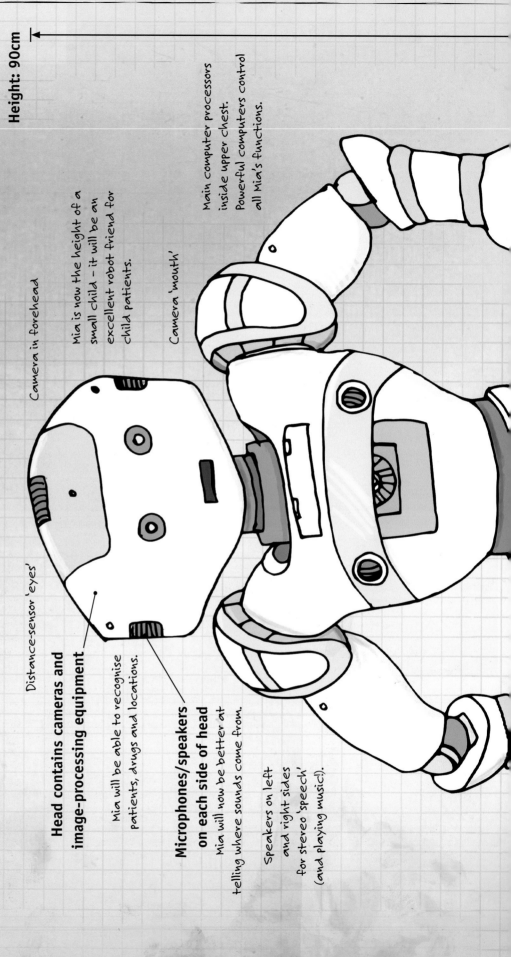

Camera in forehead

Mia is now the height of a small child – it will be an excellent robot friend for child patients.

Camera 'mouth'

Main computer processors inside upper chest. Powerful computers control all Mia's functions.

Distance-sensor 'eyes'

Head contains cameras and image-processing equipment

Mia will be able to recognise patients, drugs and locations.

Microphones/speakers on each side of head

Mia will now be better at telling where sounds come from.

Speakers on left and right sides for stereo 'speech' (and playing music!).

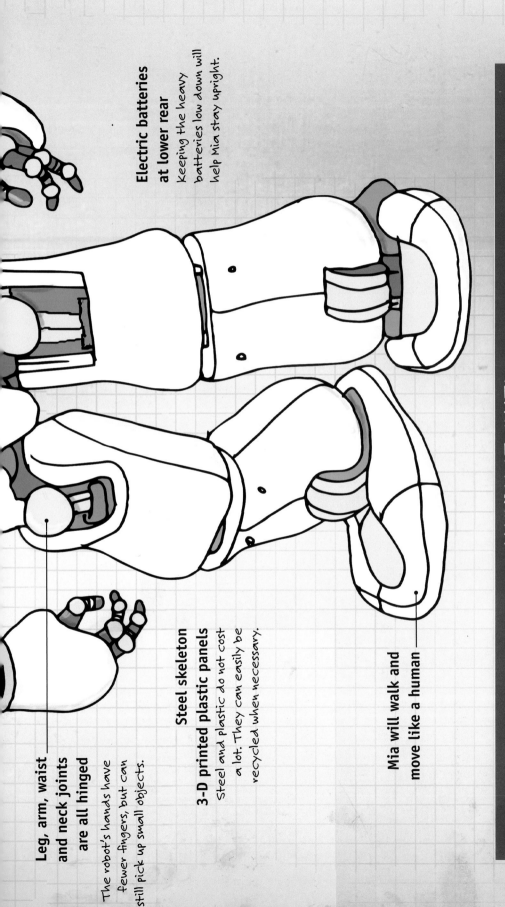

Leg, arm, waist and neck joints are all hinged

The robot's hands have fewer fingers, but can still pick up small objects.

Steel skeleton

3-D printed plastic panels

Steel and plastic do not cost a lot. They can easily be recycled when necessary.

Electric batteries at lower rear

Keeping the heavy batteries low down will help Mia stay upright.

Mia will walk and move like a human

WORK IT OUT!

People need to know about the amazing robot that could save lives!

Think about all the features and qualities that have been designed into Mia. Which three do you think will be most popular? Write them down, then make a slogan for each one.

For example:

The robot that helps people back to health!

This would tell people that Mia is designed as a healthcare robot.

Once you have three slogans, use colour and typefaces to design an eye-catching advert for Mia.

OTHER AMAZING ROBOTS

Mia is probably the world's best robot – at least for the job it is designed to do. But Mia would not be a very good combat robot, or member of a robot band. For one of those, you would need a robot designed to do the job...

COMPRESSORHEAD

RELEASED: 2013
DESIGNED AS: Robot band
This robot band has has three main members: a drummer with four arms named 'Stickboy'; a guitarist with 78 fingers ('Fingers'); and a bass-guitar player called 'Bones'.

ROBOT CAMEL JOCKEYS

DESIGNED AS: Camel-riding robots
In the United Arab Emirates, small children used to ride camels in races. This was stopped in 2002 as it was dangerous. Today, camel owners use robot jockeys instead. The robots are radio controlled by owners driving alongside in 4x4 vehicles.

SCHAFT

RELEASED: 2013
DESIGNED AS: Rescue robot
Schaft is able to work in disaster areas, such as places there has been an earthquake. It can use drills and turn doorknobs, and is as strong as 10 humans.

ChihiraAico

RELEASED: 2015
DESIGNED AS: Companion robot
ChihiraAico's designers wanted to make the robot as human as possible. It can look happy, annoyed and sad, and can even cry. Do a video search for 'ChihiraAico robot' to see if the designers succeeded.

PETMAN

RELEASED: 2013
DESIGNED AS: Tester robot
Petman was designed for testing clothing that protects soldiers against gas and other dangers. It has to be able to walk and move in the same ways as a soldier. Video-hosting sites have a funny video of Petman being tested, but with the song 'Staying Alive' as a soundtrack.

BIGDOG

RELEASED: 2008
DESIGNED AS: Military transport robot
Bigdog is the size of a very big dog, as it is 1m tall. It has four legs like a dog, and can carry a load of 150kg. Bigdog can walk on snow, ice and bumpy ground.

Bigdog packed down with supplies. It can deal with snow, ice, mud and even steep slopes.

'WORK IT OUT' ANSWERS

for p.6

Job	Skills needed
Deliver food and drink to patients	Moving around; selecting objects; passing objects to patients; possibly speaking and listening.
Give patients drugs	Moving around; recognising locations and patients, selecting objects; possibly speaking and listening.
Explain treatments to patients	Speaking and listening; responding to information.
Provide patients (especially children) with company and entertainment	Speaking and listening; responding to information; connecting to entertainment systems, such as a TV.

for p.7

1) A hospital robot really ought to look friendly, or it might scare the patients.
2) No, none of the jobs the robot will be doing needs strength.
3) A lot of smaller, cheaper robots would probably be able to do more work than one big, expensive one. Smaller robots would also be better at acting as robot friends to sick kids.

for p.11

Job	Humanoid	Tractor
Deliver food and drink to patients	1	1
Give patients drugs	1	1
Explain treatments to patients	1	0
Provide patients with company and entertainment	1	0

Skills	Humanoid	Tractor
Move about	1	1
Move objects	1	1
Recognise objects and people	1	1
Speak and listen	1	0
Process information	1	1
Sense the world around it	1	1
Look and act friendly	1	0
Be small and inexpensive	0	1

The total score is 11-8 to the humanoid shape.

for p.13

Height	86% of total height	Bedside table height	Difference
1.5m (small adult)	129cm	75cm	54cm
1.0m	86cm	75cm	11cm
0.9m	77cm	75cm	2cm
0.8m	69cm	75cm	-6cm

If the robot was 0.9m tall, its chin would be just 2cm above the height of the table top. This is the shortest height Mia should be.

for p.16

1 Walking 2 In a wheelchair 3 On a hospital trolley. As 2) and 3) both use wheels, both kinds of robot would be suitable.

for p.19

There is no correct answer, because the measurements depend on how close you were to the camera and how big the image was. The results below are just one possible answer:

Measurement	Friend 1	Friend 2	Friend 3	Max difference
1 Eye to eye	14mm	13mm	15mm	2mm
2 Chin to nose	17mm	14mm	16mm	3mm
3 Nose width	10mm	8mm	10mm	2mm
4 Mouth width	15mm	12mm	16mm	4mm
5 Ear height	11mm	8mm	9mm	3mm
6 Chin to ear lobes	17mm	20mm	18mm	3mm
7 Ear tip to ear tip	36mm	32mm	33mm	4mm

Based on these results, measurements 2, 4, 5, 6 and 7 would be the best ones for the software engineers to use.

for p.21

Fingers	Paper cup	Sandwich	Glass of water	Large orange
Fingers only	N	Y	N	N
1 finger, thumb	Y	Y	Y	N
2 fingers, thumb	Y	Y	Y	Y
3 fingers, thumb	Y	Y	Y	Y

Two fingers and a thumb would give Mia a hand that works.

for p.25

Titanium	Aluminium	Cost difference
150 x 1.8 = £270	50 x 1.8 = £90	£180

Carbon Fibre	Plastic	Cost difference
75 x 1.2 = £90	10 x 1.2 = £12	£78

The total saving from using less-expensive materials will be £258.

GLOSSARY

3-D printed made using a machine that prints out shapes from a computer design

android robot designed to look like a human

bomb disposal making a bomb harmless

bot short for robot

customised changed to fit a new brief

facial recognition identifying someone by looking at their face

flexible able to bend without breaking

function ability to do a specific task

hinge mechanism joining two objects together, which can move or bend

humanoid shaped like a human

knuckle part of a finger where two bones meet

materials what something is (or can be) made from

mono sound from one speaker

nanobot tiny robot so small that it can travel inside the human body

robotics design, building and use of robots

software instructions that control how a computer acts

stereo sound from two speakers, which seems to surround the listener

tractor robot robot that moves around on caterpillar tracks, or sometimes large wheels

uncanny valley the gap that separates something that looks not quite human (which makes it look creepy and odd) from something that looks recognisably human-like

USB short for Universal Serial Bus; a USB is a socket for attaching computers

voice recognition understanding what a person says

INDEX